CENTURIES OLD LOST SECRETS
OF **UNLEASHING** YOUR **FULL POTENTIAL**
HARNESSING THE MIND-BODY CONNECTION FOR HEALTH, WEALTH, AND HAPPINESS

MICHAEL HUANG

Copyright © 2023 Michael Huang

All rights reserved. No part of this book may be reprinted or reproduced, or utilized in any form or by any electronic, mechanical, or other means, now known or hereafter invented, including photocopying and recording, or in information storage or retrieval systems, without permission in writing from the author.

The scanning, uploading and distributing of this book via the Internet or any other means without the publisher's permission is illegal and punishable by law.

Please purchase only authorized electronic editions and do not participate in or encourage electronic piracy of copyrighted materials. Your support of the author's rights is sincerely appreciated.

Printed in the United States of America.

First Printing: 2023

"Remember: The Master Has Failed More Times Than The Beginner Has Even Tried"

~ Stephen McCranie

Dedication

A student recently gave my father and me a beautiful note with the following quote from polymath Albert Schweitzer.

"At times, our own light goes out and is rekindled by a spark from another person."

Each of us has cause to think with deep gratitude of those who have lighted the flame within us.

My inspiration and goals would only be a dream without the support of those who believe in me. I like to take this opportunity to give thanks to the following people.

My family for allowing me to do what I love — helping others through martial arts.

My father – as a child, I would watch and learn from my father before I was given the opportunity to lead. I am grateful for his unselfishness and for teaching me the value of giving.

My dreams and aspirations for relaying the torch are only meaningful because of the help from the Lifers and Inner Circle Group. Thank you for your unwavering support.

> "To laugh often and much; to win the respect of intelligent people and the affection of children; ... to appreciate beauty, to find the best in others; to leave the world a little better; whether by a healthy child or a garden patch ... to know even one life has breathed easier because you have lived. This is success."
>
> **Ralph Waldo Emerson**

Table of Contents

Introduction 1

Chapter 1   My Story 21

Chapter 2   Not Everyone Fits Us 29

Chapter 3   Start With The End In Mind 33

Chapter 4   A Lesson From The Elephant 43

Chapter 5   What's Next? 49

www.uskuoshu.com

> *"The bigger the problem you can handle, the bigger the leader you can become."*
>
> ~ Grandmaster Huang, Chien-Liang

Introduction

60 Minutes did a whole program in June 2023 about how much social media negatively impacts youth and adults.

The story is getting way too familiar:

> *Parents give their children a cell phone with the idea that it'll keep them safe. Instead, the cell phone becomes the door into a dark world, even with parental controls.*

60 Minutes shared that previously unpublished internal documents revealed that social media companies knew their platform was pushing kids to harmful content.

Parents are finally waking up, and more than 2,000 families are suing social media companies over kids' mental health.

> *"The U.S. surgeon general has called it an 'urgent public health crisis' - a devastating decline in the mental health of kids across the country. According to the CDC, the rates of suicide, self-harm, anxiety and depression are up among adolescents - a trend that began before the pandemic."*

Kids, young people, and every adult need a safe place where discipline, community, and respect are stressed.

Where social media is not celebrated and encouraged.

Where real-life human, person-to-person caring, and discipline interaction is happening. Now more than ever, our school plays a vital role where people can re-center and find balance in their lives.

My First Book

The first book I wrote was for parents who were considering enrolling their child in our martial arts school.

If I had to summarize why I wrote that book, it would be to let parents know **with certainty** that if you give us eight weeks, they would see an undeniable change in the mental and physical abilities of their child.

Off social media.

Developing self-respect and discipline.

So why did I write this second book more focused on older students and adults?

Because it doesn't matter how young or old you are, our world is focused on tearing you down, telling you why you can't do something, and just like with younger children, drawing you into a dark world.

Now more than ever, we need to get back to the mind-body connection.

It's why I chose the title for this book.

Notice I didn't say you would be a world-class martial artist.

I didn't say you would win tournaments.

I didn't say you would break boards and do perfectly executed kicks.

But what I hope you'll see as you read this book is *how everything we program in our mind has a direct relationship to our health, wealth, and happiness.*

Focus on the dark things on social media and in the news and you'll spiral down into the dark side.

But focus, instead, on the things we teach and you'll be happier, more fulfilled, and chances are more successful.

Give us 8 weeks.

Just like with our younger students, I challenge you to give us 8 weeks.

If you put in the work you won't be the same person 8 weeks later.

We don't just teach martial arts. We're much more than that. We teach life skills, life lessons – and hold our students accountable to mastering those lessons.

I will be upfront, though.

Not everyone will be accepted in our school. You must match our values of respect, discipline, and camaraderie.

If you're always late to class, won't do the out-of-class assignments, and come with a poor-me attitude, you won't be accepted at our school.

Mental and Emotional Training

It's my belief that today's students and adults need just as much (if not more) mental and emotional training – training they don't get in their regular school classroom, outside activities, or in the workplace.

> **Alex Reznikov**
> *Engineer at Alleviation Institute, LLC*
>
> How lucky it was, that we stopped by USKSA. Instantly it becomes an irreplaceable part of life. And not just for my daughter, mine as well, since I became a student too. USKSA is not just a Chinese martial arts school, it is a lifestyle. It is a family. The school changed my life I can proudly say: I am a better person now, stronger (mentally and physically), even happier than I've been before I joined the USKSA. There is not enough good words to say. Thank you.

If you are not committed to our core principle of respect and ongoing improvement, USKSA is not for you.

In ancient martial arts, students had to meet certain requirements before they would be allowed to even learn the basics with **character** being the most important.

You can walk into many martial arts studios and if you have the money to pay, they will accept you as a student.

Not here.

We still hold to the ancient belief of **the value of character.**

Why character (and life skills) are so important

Story of High Point University

I have a mentor who works directly with High Point University in North Carolina. High Point offers a range of courses that focus on developing practical life skills. These courses cover topics such as financial literacy, personal branding, communication skills, leadership development, and ethical decision-making. The aim is to equip students with the necessary skills to navigate various aspects of their personal and professional lives.

The reason they focus so much on life skills is because the president of the university, Nido Qubein, knows firsthand how important those skills are.

In fact, he teaches a class to all freshmen titled "the President's Seminar on Life Skills."

Qubein came to the U.S. as a teenager with $50 in his pocket and little English and rose as an internationally known author, consultant, speaker, and entrepreneur. In 2005, he was asked to become president of High Point and use his business knowledge and skills to transform the university.

Key to the transformation since 2005 has been the focus on not just technical training, but life-skills training.

In 2018 and again in 2022, Qubein and High Point University commissioned a survey to gain insight from executives across America on what it takes to succeed.

No matter what's happening in the world, good character and life skills ranked at the top ...

For businesses hiring employees

Being successful on the job

Getting a job promotion

Unlike High Point, most colleges focus on the technical skills of a major, and almost all ignore basic life skills.

Here's the survey's results:

- Employers believe universities across the nation are over

emphasizing technical skills over life skills (67% vs. 33%) and wish colleges would instill more life skills than technical skills (65% vs. 35%)

- 91% of employers believe that learning how to socialize outside of work is important. Employers are most concerned about hiring someone with a lack of emotional intelligence and people skills above all else (68%)

When asked by executives what is the single most important reason how someone can not only be successful in their current role but how they can move up the corporate ladder:

- 53% - Growth Mindset and strong work ethic
- 26% - Positive Attitude and working well with others
- And only 22% technical know how

When asked which attributes were likely to have employees skipped for promotion:

- 46% don't receive feedback and constructive criticism well
- 36% don't know how to solve complex problems
- And only 18% lack technical know how

USKSA is known as "The Premier Character Building and Life Skills Martial Arts School"

These kinds of skills are the reason why USKSA students go on and often become top executives.

People often say they want to be successful – live the best that life has to offer.

But they don't realize that they confuse wishful thinking with focused discipline to achieve that success.

Helping students turn wishful thinking into confident, successful adults with highly developed life skills is what makes us unique.

I've seen student after student walk through our doors and succeed beyond their wildest imagination.

Why?

Because we have over 50 years of working with students to not only create elite athletes but also to turn on their

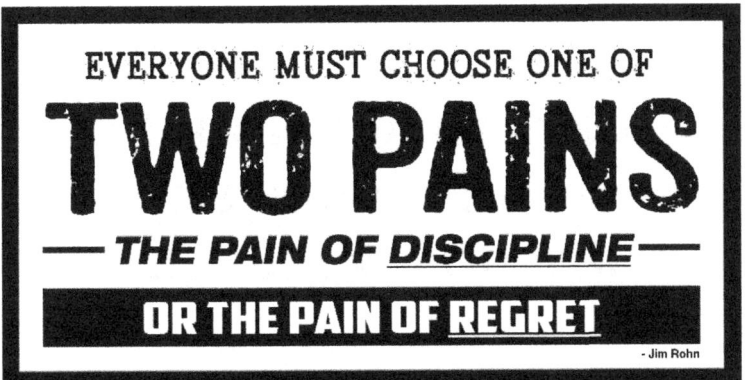

God-given belief system and core values resulting in uncommon success stories.

Truth #1: Every successful achievement begins with a decision

You can get ordinary at many other options out there (including other martial art schools).

But here we teach — and expect — all our students to not only grow physically as they learn traditional Chinese Kung Fu (Kuo Shu), but we also focus on developing the students' minds, bodies, and spirits to set them on a course for life-long success.

It took me nearly 20 years to develop the character values and life lessons we teach.

That's two decades of doing mat lessons (also called mat chats) week after week and fine-tuning until we're known internationally as developing elite, well-rounded students.

Many people have the idea that martial artists are under-educated and have no other options.

They would be wrong.

Especially at our school.

Many top executives, professionals, and leaders seek martial arts training.

Why?

Because even if you have all the money in the world, there is no better investment than investing in yourself. No amount of money can buy health and skill; you have to train and train with the best.

These days I focus primarily on the advanced students, but I am always careful to see how the younger students are doing under the guidance of my well-trained instructors.

This is not the easy button

I will be upfront with you.

What I teach in our martial arts school is not easy.

You will be tested both physically and mentally.

If you're looking for the easy button, you should probably close this book and move on. I'm not for you.

But ...

If you are looking for a life-changing, life-altering experience, and training — and you match our values — then I respectfully encourage you to take the 30 minutes it will take to read this book.

I kept it short on purpose.

You can't really know how you will grow and change until you come week after week and experience the growth and change all our students experience.

We only focus on helping you understand that, many times, your self-defeating, limiting beliefs are in your own head.

We focus on what Carol Dweck (Author of *Growth Mindset* and professor of psychology at Stanford University) refers to as a "growth mindset." A mindset where abilities are not set in stone.

Instead, with the proper mindset and guidance, you can develop your skills over time and be quite competent in any subject.

You CAN do things you thought were impossible

- We focus on our students knowing their strengths and value.
- We focus on respect for authority figures.
- We focus on responsibility.

- We focus on the ability to calm the mind and know one's true worth.

- We focus on life skills.

- We focus on no excuses.

- We focus on gratitude.

GRATITUDE

And have we succeeded with our students?

I think you'll find the answer to that question in the stories I've scattered throughout this book. I would also

www.uskuoshu.com

encourage you to check out more stories on our website at www.USKuoShu.com.

These stories have been passed down by my father and then through me over the 50 years of our students living successful lives. Many have even risen as executives in top organizations in the country.

Thank you for taking the 30-minute journey with me to read this book. I'm hoping in the end you'll agree that it makes sense to schedule a free evaluation lesson.

Let's get started!

Master Michael Huang

Chapter 1

My Story

I've spent my entire life involved with martial arts under the guidance of my father, Grandmaster Huang, Chien-Liang.

When your father is a world-class Grandmaster, daily life becomes ongoing lessons through a martial arts lens.

My father was born in Malaysia and began his martial arts training at the age of 12. By age 19, he had moved to Taiwan to attend the university and began studying with his Shi Ye, Supreme

Master Wang, Chueh-Jen (王玨鑫). (For those unfamiliar with the term, "Shi Ye" is the traditional reference for a teacher of Northern Chinese martial arts.)

In 1972, he was invited to move to America and teach Kung Fu, and 3 years later, he had an opportunity to open his own Tien Sun Wushu school in Ohio while continuing his own training under Shi Ye.

In his school, he focused on teaching a more traditional way of martial arts combined with the development of good character: respect, loyalty, humility, and compassion.

All success traits.

All ancient martial arts traits.

Since then, we have taught and promoted Chinese martial arts in over 30 countries and were fortunate to be ranked as one of the most impactful martial arts in the 20th century by *Inside Kung-Fu* because of our student success and contribution in martial arts.

My father has been referred to as a *Maker of Champions and Builder of Character.*

Because of him, we have started schools in Europe, the U.S., and South America.

Our students ...

- Believe they can, and they do
- Eliminate excuses
- Become bold and confident and destroy fear in their lives
- Think BIG
- Take the right action
- Turn defeat into victory

- Become confident leaders
- Treat everyone with respect

Truth #2: Your main opponent in Kung Fu is always yourself

We have hundreds of testimonials about changed lives (many of whom you'll read about in this book).

They change:

- Physically
- Mentally
- Emotionally

They learn:

- Mental toughness
- How to overcome challenges

- And think strategically – multiple steps ahead of everyone else

They:

- Do better in their jobs
- Find jobs easier
- Get promoted faster

A large percentage of our students go on and become top executives and are very successful in their careers.

They come to the school thinking they will get physically fit. They find that the community of like-minded, focused students and teachers is unlike anything they've ever experienced anywhere else and becomes a life-changing experience.

My Early Years Post College

I started a different career path from my father, I went to college and graduated from the business school at the University of Maryland, landing a job right out of school with a high-end investment firm.

The most valuable thing I received from that job was being able to learn the mindset and thinking of one of the top investors in the country.

How he thought.

How he reacted.

How he looked at the pros and cons of anything he was doing.

It was a great learning environment, but when my hours kept getting longer and longer, and having gained 50 pounds, I knew it was time to return to my martial arts roots.

I took the lessons I learned from the master investor and implemented them into our elite martial arts school.

It is the best of both worlds.

Top mindset combined with Chinese martial arts!

Martial arts is not a hobby for me — it's a way of life, and that is why our school is anything but ordinary.

In the next chapter, you learn that we are not for everyone, and we only work with those students/families who match our values.

Andria Yu
Director of Media Relations at Motorcycle Industry Council

This Is Truly A Traditional Chinese Martial Arts School.

I've been studying at U.S. Kuo Shu Academy for about six years now, and I am so impressed by the depth of knowledge that the instructors at this school have. This is truly a traditional Chinese martial arts school.

I have been learning Tai Ji Quan from this school, and it's exactly the type of Tai Ji I was looking for. Not just the basic stuff you learn from a community center or gym, but true in-depth knowledge of the martial aspects of tai chi and how it builds the inner energy, the chi. There's meditation, Qi Gong and weapons work, too!

Everyone at the school is so supportive of the students and of one another. And you not only learn martial arts, you learn ways to become the best version of yourself.

Chapter 2

Not Everyone Fits Us

Martial arts has always been focused on developing discipline. And our school is no different. It is a key factor to success.

However, we go far beyond the traditional martial arts school. In the last chapter, I shared that it's taken me 20 years to develop the life success curriculum for our students.

It wasn't an overnight burst of inspiration. It was developed through what we call "mat chats" with over 20 classes a week, night after night, year after year.

All the time, refining and fine-tuning what I taught beyond the martial arts lessons.

Why would I do that?

Why would I not just take the latest shiny object being taught at the martial arts national conventions like most instructors would do?

Because I never saw anything out there that comes close to developing elite students like what my father and I have developed over the years.

And testimony after testimony from our students who have become our best advertising says it all.

Change can start at any age

Whether a student comes in as a young person or walks in as an adult, the lesson of respect, loyalty, and compassion are fundamental to our black sash program (I'll talk about that in the next chapter).

Every student is required to memorize our two creeds:

> ### USKSA Student Creed
> - I will develop myself physically, mentally, and emotionally based on the TSP motto.
> - I will only use my kung fu as a last resort.
> - I will do the best I can by not making excuses.
> - I will be honest and compassionate to myself and others.
> - I will earn my black sash.

> ### Tien Shan Pai Creed
> Kuo Shu begins and ends with respect. As a dedicated Tien Shan Pai student, I will live by the motto and principles of a Tien San Pai black sash.
>
> Respect ♦ Loyalty ♦ Righteousness ♦ Compassion

In today's culture, everyone has their phones in their hand and playing games, surfing the web, or chatting on social media. And even worse – spiraling down the dark path I talked about in the introduction.

Attention spans have gone down and peer pressure to follow the wrong path is getting stronger all the time.

Which is why one of the things we teach is the 4 laws of concentration. No highly successful person gets there continually distracted.

Part of our sash system is to eliminate some of the distractions and help you create new healthier habits.

Get off social media

Turn TV news off

Change your diet

The end goal at our school is to reach "Black Sash Leadership," which is what I talk about in the next chapter.

Chapter 3
Start With The End In Mind

It was Stephen Covey, in his book, *Seven Principles of Highly Effective People,* who said,

"Always start with the end in mind."

I agree.

This is why whenever new students start with us, we focus on the end goal: **Black Sash**.

You might have heard of martial arts schools using colored ranking belts, with a black belt being the highest. In our school, we use sashes, but the concepts are the same.

Everything we do is focused on the psychology of achieving the top prize (e.g., the black sash).

To earn a black sash, students must apply the mental and emotional skills of:

- Short- and long-term goal setting
- Creating habits of focus, discipline, and follow through
- Overcoming negative peer pressure
- Respect for authority

These skills must be learned and demonstrated, both in and out of class, before a student earns a Black Sash.

It doesn't matter if the student is still in elementary school or if the student is an adult already working.

The goal is the same: to become a Black Sash.

You will often hear me say "WE ARE A BLACK SASH SCHOOL!"

Truth #3: A BLACK SASH always thinks about the next step toward their goal.

When students come for the first time, they start with an Evaluation Lesson.

The purpose of our Evaluation Lesson is to prepare a student to set a goal to BLACK SASH & BEYOND!

- Your instructors will be looking to see *if you qualify for U.S. Kuo Shu Academy's (USKSA's) Black Sash Leadership Program.*

- This process can take AS LITTLE as 4-8 weeks. However, it may take longer, depending on the dedication and attitude you show in your training.

- You will be invited to continue into Black Sash Leadership only if you show us you are serious about applying the Black Sash habits and attitudes you learn in class.

It's the #1 reason our students excel in life and their careers.

They're expected to break through limiting beliefs and excel!!! And they do.

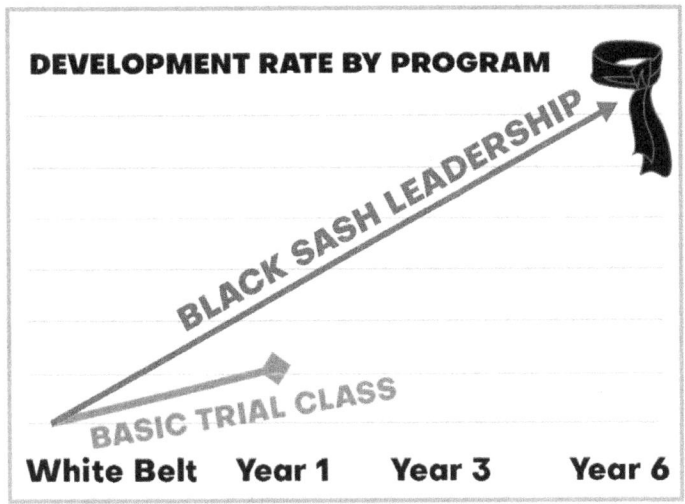

We are a "No Excuses" school.

The purpose of the Evaluation Lesson is to give you an overview of the school.

From there, your main objective is to qualify for our Black Sash Leadership Program.

It doesn't even matter if you have attention problems or disabilities.

If you are committed to supporting our value-based curriculum, we welcome **all** students.

Truth #4: Part of being a good martial arts practitioner means being able to limit or put aside distractions in order to achieve greater clarity and presence of mind.

"We Highly Recommend U.S. Kuo Shu Academy to Students of All Ages."

My children and I have been privileged and honored to train with Grandmaster Huang for many years through numerous seminars. The opportunity to train with him is INVALUABLE given his wealth of KNOWLEDGE and DEDICATION in traditional Chinese martial arts, focusing on mind, body & spirit. We have known Grandmaster Huang, Master Michael Huang, and their instructor staff for more than 14 years, and we hold them in the highest regard. Their dedication to martial arts and their students is exceptional. We highly recommend U.S. Kuo Shu Academy to students of all ages who are interested in authentic and high-quality martial arts training for themselves and/or their family members.

Janice Fitzsimmons
Bok Fu Do Black Belt

In the next chapter, I will share the biggest lesson our students must first learn.

If you give up before your goal has been reached, you are a "Quitter"

A QUITTER NEVER WINS AND A WINNER NEVER QUITS

— Napoleon Hill

"Your outlook upon life, estimate of yourself and estimate of your value are largely colored by your environment. Your whole career will be modified, shaped and molded by your surroundings and the character of the people with whom you come into contact every day."

Orison Swett Marden,
Founder of Success Magazine

SEVEN WORDS OF RESPECT

Yes Sir
Yes Ma'am
No Sir
No Ma'am
Thank You
You're Welcome
Please

Alyssa Shedlosky
Associate Director, R&D Hardware Engineering at BD

I Highly Recommend This School.

My sons and I have been at USKSA for over two years training in Kung Fu and Tai Ji Quan. It's a wonderful community of people and the classes are great with a variety of self-defenses, sparring, forms with and without weapons, and meditation. There's so much to learn and you'll see and feel the progression within just a few weeks but never get bored for years to come.

Best of all, there's a place for everyone - no matter your abilities. Each person is physically and mentally challenged in their own ways and USKSA really promotes that this is your journey to take and they're there to support you. I highly recommend this school so stop wondering whether to sign up and just do it!

Chapter 4

A Lesson From The Elephant

Elephants are one of the largest and most powerful creatures on earth. They could crush anything or anyone in their way, but when you go to the zoo or circus, you see them sitting quietly, held only by a small chain or rope.

How is this possible?

Because of "elephant chaining."

When an elephant is a baby, they are tied down with chains (or ropes) that are too strong for them to break through.

They will struggle and try, but they can never break the chain and get free.

As they try, the chain will tear into their skin, causing pain. The pain causes them to stop trying.

As they grow, their trainers can use smaller and smaller chains to hold them, and they eventually will never try to break free again.

No matter how weak the chain or rope is, the elephant will not try to break it.

It's a lesson for every one of us.

From very young, we are told NO and trained to avoid trying to do the "impossible."

Why don't we

- Try out for a class play?
- Study hard to get the top grade on a test?
- Apply for that job?
- Ask that special person on a date?

It's because somewhere in the past, we were chained to the belief that we couldn't do it, weren't good enough, or got burned once trying.

We gave up because, "Why try the impossible?"

We slip into a pattern of only trying things we perceive as easy and achievable. We never stretch, we simply accept a life of mediocrity.

This is why our Black Sash martial arts training is life-changing for students.

We challenge students to overcome their fears and insecurities and realize they can do the impossible.

I once read a story of a teacher who told a group of students they had above-average intelligence and would be moved into an advanced class.

They were told they were highly gifted and special.

In reality, they just tested average, but they didn't know it.

If they knew they were average, they could have had excuses like:

- The work will be too hard.

- I'm not smart enough.

- There's no way I can make it in that class.

But because they were told they were above average, they all excelled.

In fact, ALL of them ended up with A's and B's.

It was simply an issue of their belief — never an issue of their intelligence.

A chained mindset can be the biggest obstacle to lifelong success.

We teach our Black Sash students the benefits of tugging on that chain and breaking through.

The only way they fail is by not trying.

It all starts with a plan.

"The Instructors Are All Top Notch, Professional and Truly Care About Each and Every Student."

My son and I are both students at USKSA and it has been an awesome experience for us. I've really enjoyed watching my son DEVELOP DISCIPLINE and RESPECT while learning the fundamentals of Tien Shan Pai. The instructors are all top-notch, professional and truly care about each and every student. In addition to learning Kung Fu, my flexibility, endurance and coordination have all greatly improved. I'm very pleased with my experience and would recommend USKSA to anyone!

Ray Ro

Chapter 5

What's Next?

First, I'd like to thank you for reading this short book.

I purposely kept it short because, while I can tell you about our history and why we're different, and the benefits of enrolling in our Evaluation Lesson, until you

- actually experience it,
- watch us in action and
- see what we require of you

you won't truly know the reason why we are an elite school that is trusted by high-profile students.

This is why I have a "Prove It to Me, Michael" offer.

Call my school at 443-394-9222 and tell us you'd like to attend an Evaluation Lesson.

We'll get you scheduled.

No Risk to You!!

I will take all the risk and invite you to come *for free* the first time to see if we'll be a fit. (No … I don't accept everyone who wants to join our Black Sash program.)

You must match our values and be committed to your weekly assignments.

Give us a call at 443-394-9222, and let's get you started.

I'm honored to work with every student to teach character values while at the same time teaching martial arts disciplines.

I'm looking forward to seeing your name on the class schedule.

Master Michael Huang

www.uskuoshu.com

★ ★ ★ ★ ★

"The Best School of Martial Arts"

Irvin Lee
Parent of two at U.S. Kuo Shu Academy

My children have been students for more than 4 years now and they love this school of martial arts. US Kuo Shu Academy is their second home, learning not just kung fu but also developing one's character as good, responsible, respectful and disciplined citizen. Thank you very much Grandmaster Huang, Master Michael Huang and all the teachers and students for making this place the best school of martial arts.

★ ★ ★ ★ ★

"What I learn here directly translates to how I approach every challenge I've had with school or otherwise."

Mitchell Jay
Graduate of Yale University and BethTfiloh Congregation & Community School

I started taking lessons at US Kuo Shu Academy when I was five years old. Each aspect of my USKSA training has helped me navigate... challenges inside and outside martial arts. I can attribute nearly all of my achievements, from earning my black sash and competing in Lei Tai to graduating college and applying to medical school, to the USKSA. Each goal has built on itself and helped me with the other, creating a large web of goals that are intimately related and cannot be separated; every opportunity to teach, push myself, and realize my potential in Kung Fu has also helped me maintain self-confidence outside of martial arts. There is no better investment for your physical, mental and emotional well-being.

★ ★ ★ ★ ★

"Nothing Short of Amazing."

Margaret Boas
Professor at Anne Arundel Community College

The US Kuo Shu Academy is an amazing, traditional martial arts school with stellar instructors and an incredibly well-developed curriculum. My experience there - both at Owings Mills and in Marriottsville - has been nothing short of amazing. The Tai Chi program provides an incredibly layered experience that combines both the meditative/health aspects of Tai Chi, along with the martial aspects of the form. They truly care about their students, and provide expertise and support in an environment that is both caring and rigorous. Whether your interest in Tai Chi or Kung Fu, meditation or martial practice, this is the place to be.

★ ★ ★ ★ ★

"Becoming a student at U.S. Kuo Shu Academy changed my life in many ways."

Shelly Henriquez-Neill
Executive Coach and Leadership Consultant

Becoming a student at U.S Kuo Shu Academy changed my life in many ways. The lessons I've learned here and continue to learn here are rooted in martial arts principles yes, but are also deeply reflective of life and the principles of living a balanced and a good life. Although I'm an instructor now, I'm always a student first. It's easy to love being a student when you have amazing teachers. The gatekeepers of my greatest lessons in martial arts have been Grandmaster Huang, Master Huang, Master Chisholm, Master Green, and all the Shi Fus and training partners I have had the honor to know since being here. The quality of my friendships since I first joined have changed, my physical frame and my level of fitness has changed in at least three different ways over the years, my awareness and ability to control my mindset and adjust when faced with triggers or upset has developed tremendously. I met the love of my life I got married and we are building a life together that I had once only dreamed of. Being a student of Tien Shan Pai means that I'm always doing my best to honor and live by the school motto of virtue, wisdom, humility, and martial arts. As I continue to study the art, my goal for black sash and beyond is to help people by inspiring the spirit of resilience, authenticity, integrity, and joy.

★ ★ ★ ★ ★

"It becomes a place that you can have joy, that you can actually have camaraderie, that you actually are able to reset and feel good about the world."

Michelle Santos
Chief Creative Officer at Richard Wright Public Charter School

At my job I started as a coordinator, then a director and now I am a chief. It was in the same timeline as my growth here and getting my black sash, and it continues to grow. I have to say that it has been exponential to how this school, this environment, this practice, this discipline has contributed to my life, to my family, and so, I just want to whole heartedly thank everybody, thank you Master Huang, thank you to all my teachers because you had an enormous impact. Even when we go through the different struggles in our lives, this place becomes like a safe haven. It becomes a place that you can have joy, that you can actually have camaraderie, that you actually are able to reset and feel good about the world. Thank you for just being a part of my journey.

www.uskuoshu.com

★ ★ ★ ★ ★

"The school has transformed my life."

Bruce Seward
Logistics Specialist

The school has transformed my life and made me a better man body and soul. It's really special to witness the transformation of the youth at the school as well. The staff at the school really care about the students and each other. This is all so vital to our youth for they are the future of things to come.

If you're not ready to take the next step, watch our "ABOUT US" video to learn more about us.